The California Gold Rush

A Captivating Guide to One of the Most Significant Events in the History of the United States of America and Its Impact on Native American Tribes

© Copyright 2021

All Rights Reserved. No part of this book may be reproduced in any form without permission in writing from the author. Reviewers may quote brief passages in reviews.

Disclaimer: No part of this publication may be reproduced or transmitted in any form or by any means, mechanical or electronic, including photocopying or recording, or by any information storage and retrieval system, or transmitted by email without permission in writing from the publisher.

While all attempts have been made to verify the information provided in this publication, neither the author nor the publisher assumes any responsibility for errors, omissions, or contrary interpretations of the subject matter herein.

This book is for entertainment purposes only. The views expressed are those of the author alone, and should not be taken as expert instruction or commands. The reader is responsible for his or her own actions.

Adherence to all applicable laws and regulations, including international, federal, state, and local laws governing professional licensing, business practices, advertising, and all other aspects of doing business in the US, Canada, UK, or any other jurisdiction is the sole responsibility of the purchaser or reader.

Neither the author nor the publisher assumes any responsibility or liability whatsoever on the behalf of the purchaser or reader of these materials. Any perceived slight of any individual or organization is purely unintentional.

Free Bonus from Captivating History (Available for a Limited time)

Hi History Lovers!

Now you have a chance to join our exclusive history list so you can get your first history ebook for free as well as discounts and a potential to get more history books for free! Simply visit the link below to join.

Captivatinghistory.com/ebook

Also, make sure to follow us on Facebook, Twitter and Youtube by searching for Captivating History.

Contents

INTRODUCTION 1
CHAPTER 1 – THE DISCOVERY OF GOLD 3
CHAPTER 2 – GOING TO CALIFORNIA 10
CHAPTER 3 – THE LABOR FORCE 18
CHAPTER 4 – WOMEN IN THE CALIFORNIA GOLD RUSH 26
CHAPTER 5 – THE GOLDEN STATE 33
CHAPTER 6 – THE SIGNIFICANCE OF THE CALIFORNIA GOLD RUSH ON THE GLOBAL ECONOMY 38
CONCLUSION 42
HERE'S ANOTHER BOOK BY CAPTIVATING HISTORY THAT YOU MIGHT LIKE 44
FREE BONUS FROM CAPTIVATING HISTORY (AVAILABLE FOR A LIMITED TIME) 45
REFERENCES 46

Introduction

In January 1848, when James Marshall noticed the first glimmer of gold at the bottom of the millrace, he didn't even dream he would change the history of the world. He had discovered gold at the bottom of the river of a new United States frontier, California.

In the years that followed, the newly acquired territory swelled with people rushing to make a fortune. California had previously been under the governance of Mexico. Although it was known that the Mexicans did some gold mining in the region, the European-Americans needed a bigger motivation to start settling in California. This motivation was provided by the discovery of gold, as newspapers rushed to exaggerate, promising that the gold was there for the taking. Only then did tens of thousands of people set on a journey to the West. But it wasn't only Americans who were struck with gold fever. Many miners came from Great Britain, China, Australia, South America, and other countries from around the world.

During the early years of the California Gold Rush, most of the people headed directly to the rivers. These first brave men and women are remembered in history as the forty-niners or the Argonauts, and there are many tales about their heroism, their struggles to settle in the wild western territories, and their troubles with the Native Americans. However, all these stories are heavily romanticized, and they do not tell historical events from an objective perspective.

The romantic stories of the Gold Rush pioneers disregard the violence, poverty, and famine that happened to the indigenous peoples of California. The arrival of European-Americans and Europeans sealed the fate of the Native Americans living in California. Even the US government approved mass killings and the relocations that followed. Although the period of the California Gold Rush is of extreme importance for the development of the United States of America, history should never tell a one-sided story. This is not only the tale of how the discovery of gold lifted the US to the top of the world's economies. This is also a story of society, laborers, the first immigrant laws, women and their role in the mining societies, slavery and freedom, and statehood. Finally, this is a story of genocide, of Native Americans who were forced to abandon their ancestral homes and relocate to designated reservations.

Chapter 1 – The Discovery of Gold

Gold panning
https://en.wikipedia.org/wiki/California_Gold_Rush#/media/File:Gull graver_1850_California.jpg

Only twenty years after the adoption of the Declaration of Independence in 1776, the United States expanded its territory and doubled its size. After another fifty years, the expansion reached across the plains, mountains, fields, and deserts, all the way to the Pacific coast. During the Mexican-American War (1846–1848), the US Army conquered the territory of Alta California, which allowed them to invade Baja California. When the war ended in 1848, California (among others) became a part of the United States under the terms set by the Treaty of Guadalupe Hidalgo. This expansion of US territory was President James K. Polk's vision, although many contemporaries criticized him for starting the war with Mexico. When Polk was near the end of his presidency, he addressed the nation on December 5th, 1848. He spoke of California, and the nation eagerly listened, waiting for the confirmation of the existence of gold. But what made the whole nation wait for such news? Why were they explicitly interested in hearing about California?

A single event occurred on January 24th, 1848. In the Sierra Nevada Hills, A carpenter from New Jersey, James W. Marshall, was building a water-driven sawmill when he found glittering gold in the river. At that time, Marshall wasn't sure what he found, and he thought it wise to consult his employer, a Swiss immigrant who had big dreams of starting a cattle farm in the new land. This immigrant's name was John Sutter (Johann Sutter), who came to California in 1839 after fleeing imprisonment in his home country due to unpaid debts. He became a Mexican citizen (at this time, California was a part of Mexico) and settled on a 48,000-acre ranch, which was granted to him by the Mexican government. In return, John Sutter promised he would curtail American efforts to take parts of California. He named this land New Helvetia, but instead of safeguarding the border against the American intrusions, he often helped the US migrants settle in the territory of Mexico.

When Sutter learned about the gold nugget his employee Marshall had found, he decided to test it. After all, he couldn't be sure if it was indeed gold. Together, Marshall and Sutter found information on how to test gold in an old encyclopedia. First, they pounded the golden nugget between two rocks. The nugget flattened but didn't break, a positive sign that they were holding gold. Then, they tested it in nitric acid, which would affect most metals except for gold. Still, they were not completely satisfied with the results, and they conducted one more test. They placed the nugget on a scale and counterweighted it with three silver coins. Then, they submerged the scales under the water. The side that contained the nugget sank, as gold had a higher density than silver. Finally, their suspicions were confirmed. They were sure they had found gold!

Their timing was very important, as this all happened only nine days before California became a part of the United States. Sutter was resolved to keep the discovery of gold quiet because he feared that his own cattle farm business would fail. He dreamed of building a farming empire, and the big influx of people that would come to mine the gold, as well as the landscape changes that would occur during the mining process, would bring down his industry. Sutter was right because once the Gold Rush began, his business suffered. But to prevent it, the first thing Sutter did was rush to confirm he owned the land on which the gold was found. Since California still belonged to Mexico, he had to file documents with the Mexican authorities. But the land he owned was on Coloma territory, and Mexico declined his claim on the land because, under the law, native peoples were not allowed to grant leases.

And even though Sutter tried, it was impossible to keep the news away from the public. A Mormon store owner and publisher named Samuel Brannan visited Sutter's Mill, and there, he acquired gold nuggets by trading with Sutter's Mormon workers. Upon his return to San Francisco, he started publishing news about his findings. But Brannan was also the owner of a store in San Francisco and a visionary. He predicted the start of the Gold Rush, for which he pushed. He bought all the gold-searching equipment, such as picks, pans, and shovels, he could get his hands on. He would resell them for an enormous price while urging people to go to Sutter's land. In just nine weeks, Brannan earned more than $36,000. Taking into account the inflation rate since 1848, Brannan made approximately the equivalent of $1,200,000. He was the first person to become a millionaire from the California Gold Rush. But the rush hadn't yet started. People, in general, tended not to believe the journalists, especially the ones who settled in the new western territories. They believed that the claims about gold were just rumors.

While the journalist prospered, the Swiss entrepreneur Sutter suffered. The people rushed to his land and destroyed everything he had managed to build. The whole of San Francisco moved toward Sutter's farm. When the news hit Monterey, every soldier, sailor, and merchant was hit by gold fever. They, too, left for Sutter's land. Once there, they killed his cattle and burned buildings. Sutter lost everything except what little gold he had managed to find. Sutter managed to salvage some of his business and land, and he transferred the ownership to his eldest son. But the family lost their fortune, and their debt was increasing. Even though Sutter Junior started in Sacramento City in the vicinity of the family estate, he was forced to sell the land to pay off the debt. He then moved to Acapulco, Mexico. One of the businessmen who obtained this land was Samuel Brannan, the journalist who had started it all.

The people were already coming to California hoping to find gold, trusting the rumors of its discovery, before Polk's speech even took place. But the Gold Rush only truly began with his speech on December 5th, 1848. Polk explained that it was known that Mexicans had extracted gold in California before the territory was ceded to the US. However, the extent of the gold veins and their value and purity were unknown. The field reports Polk received from the public service officials who visited California during that year confirmed the abundance of gold. The whole nation listened and celebrated. The civilians were sure the gold was there for the taking, while the politicians congratulated Polk for adding California's gold deposits to the national inventory of natural resources. Even Polk's critics had to admit that the value of California was worth the war.

But, at first, even Polk was reluctant to trust the news of the discovery of gold. Three separate messengers were sent to him from California's military governor Richard Mason. One left on August 30th, 1848, by boat, through the Isthmus of Panama. This man arrived in Washington in November. The second one left on September 13th, and he traveled overland, crossing Mexico. He also arrived in Washington in November. The third and the fastest messenger was sent by land, but he managed to arrive in Washington on September 18th. It was only after receiving these three messages and three samples of gold that President Polk started believing in California's gold resources. The speech he held concerning California was just a spark, but the newspapers took over and exaggerated the stories, feeding the flame.

The *New York Herald* was the first publication on the East Coast to publish the discovery of gold in California. The people started rushing to the West in hopes of gaining wealth. San Francisco was only a small town of barely two hundred inhabitants when Samuel Brannan walked its streets, yelling, "Gold, gold in the rivers of America!" At the end of 1848, it already counted one thousand inhabitants, and over the next two years, it grew to house twenty-five thousand residents. In just four years after the announcement of the discovery, California's population increased from 14,000 to 250,000. But it wasn't only the number of inhabitants that changed almost overnight. It was also the composition of the population. Before California became a part of the United States, the majority of the population was Hispanic (around 80 percent). The Native Americans, who saw a decrease in their numbers over time, counted around 150,000 souls.

The population change had already started when California was ceded, as many people moved from the East Coast to the newly gained territory in hopes of gaining some land and starting farms. But it was not until the Gold Rush that the change in population composition started hurting the Hispanic and Native American populations. From 1849 until 1870, the Hispanics dropped from 80 percent to only 4 percent. Even though at that time California numbered around 380,000 people, only 31,000 were Native Americans. But it wasn't only US citizens who were rushing to California to extract its gold. There were many Chileans, Peruvians, French, British, Chinese, Japanese, and even Australians who were struck by the gold fever. Together with the Americans of the East Coast, they pushed the Native Americans from their land, away from their hunting grounds and natural resources. The new settlers brought diseases with them that Native Americans never experienced before. They had no immunity developed against them, and many of them succumbed to simple diseases such as the flu. But many more Native Americans were deprived of their land or killed.

When all the gold from the rivers was picked, and the only remaining sources were deep underground, mining became the only solution to acquiring gold. But to mine on the land that still belonged to Native Americans was impossible. So, the US government sought to remove the remaining native peoples. State legislature soon gave the new settlers in California the right to take custody of Native American children, thus effectively allowing slavery. Laws also gave the settlers the right to arrest Native Americans for any minor offenses, such as the possession of alcohol. The convicted natives had to work off their sentences. In the name of "protection," tens of thousands of natives were enslaved. Yet, this was just the beginning. The government wanted to resolve the "Indian problem" quickly, and they instigated hatred toward the native peoples. The settlers were convinced they couldn't get their hands on the gold before they removed the Native Americans, so they started slaughtering them. The government turned a blind eye to the violence and even started funding the local militias against the native tribes. Those Native Americans who tried to resist and fight back were poorly armed and had no experience in fighting with guns. They stood no chance against the whites. Local officials put bounties on Native American heads, urging the settlers to start massacres.

Chapter 2 – Going to California

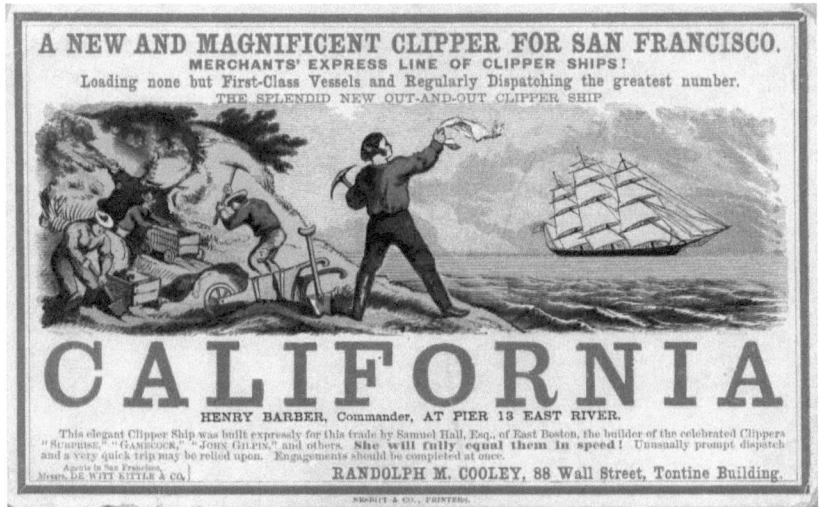

Advertisement on sailing to California from 1850

https://en.wikipedia.org/wiki/California_Gold_Rush#/media/File:California_Clipper_500.jpg

Before the Gold Rush, those who wanted to settle in the West would go toward Oregon's Willamette Valley. But after the discovery of gold at Sutter's sawmill, the Oregon Trail was changed forever. Thousands of wagons, carrying people, supplies, and equipment, poured into the Sierra Nevada, from where they would descend to Sacramento Valley.

But in 1848, only around four hundred California-bound people were on this road. The very next year, that number climbed to thirty thousand. The Gold Rush pioneers were called "forty-niners" because they started their journey to California in 1849. Alternatively, they were called the "Argonauts," after the Greek myth about Jason and his ship, the *Argo*. In this myth, the heroes were chasing for the golden fleece of a magical ram, and with the help of the gods, they managed to find it.

But the road to the West was harsh, and the crowded paths became the resting place of many dead animals, discarded personal belongings, and wagon parts. Just in 1850, over two thousand wagons, horses, and mules were abandoned in the desert of California. One month after President Polk's speech, over sixty ships, filled with people eager to get to California, left the ports of the East Coast. Whaling ships were turned into passenger ships because the demand was so high that it was profitable to charge the people for transport rather than to hunt whales. But these ships were not well maintained for the most part, and they were in no condition to carry so many people. They sank before reaching San Francisco. Clipper ships, designed for speed, were the fastest, and they could reach California in only three months. But they were also the most expensive option. Time was money; the sooner you got to California, the more chances you had to find gold and to survive the hardship of the journey. The slowest were paddle-wheel steamer ships. They took almost a year to reach California. On average, a settler would travel for 115 days, starting in New York or Boston.

There were two sea routes to California. The first one went south from the East Coast, traveling the Atlantic to the Horn of Hope, around South America, reaching the Pacific, and then climbing north toward California. The second route went south to the Isthmus of Panama, where they had to then traverse the jungle with horses or mules for at least a week and catch a ship for California on the Pacific side of the Isthmus of Panama. The third route was completely by land, and it started at Independence, St. Joseph, or St. Louis, Missouri. The men would buy oxen and covered wagons, which they used to carry supplies and equipment. They would ride on horses next to the wagons. They also took passengers, who either occupied very limited space in the wagons or chose to walk next to the wagons. Traveling along the land route was very slow and exhausting. Some of them chose to turn south, which was known as the Santa Fe Trail. Then, they would turn toward California, the so-called Old Spanish Trail. Some forty-niners decided to take a boat to Texas, then ride or walk through Mexico to San Diego. This was known as the Sonora Trail.

Most of the people who were struck by the gold fever were poor, and to afford the trip to California, they had to sell everything they owned. Many of them even borrowed the money from their relatives, friends, or banks so they could pay for a ship ticket. They counted on getting rich from the gold they would find, which would allow them to pay off their debts. The average cost of the trip was around $1,000. But the minimum spending for the whole trip was around $750 per person. There were many dangers on the road, such as wild animals and bandits, so the Argonauts had to carry arms. They had at least a revolver and a knife, but rifles and shotguns were carried too. Some cases are known where walking sticks would turn into swords, batons, or blackjacks. The weapons also served hunting purposes or to shoot what little cattle the people brought with them. They were also used to protect one's claims to land and to shoot Native Americans, who would attack settlers on their way to the West.

But some of the biggest nuisances on the road to California were the robbers. Some were murderers, while others would take money and valuables but leave their victims alive. There were also thieves, gamblers, tricksters, and fraudsters. Some of them were even romanticized, and from their adventures, many legends have sprouted. The most famous legend is about Joaquin Murrieta. It is not known if he was a real person, as there is no firm evidence of his existence. There is one known case of horse theft committed by someone of that name but nothing else. The legend grew to immense proportions, and Joaquin became famous as California's Robin Hood. He wasn't simply a bandit but was on a path of revenge. He defeated all the Anglo settlers who accused him and his brother of horse theft and those who killed his young wife. According to the legend, the government had to put a bounty on his head, and Joaquin was eventually caught and killed.

Many people were killed on the road, some by robbers and Native Americans, but most died of various diseases. Cholera was the biggest problem. One traveler noted how in one day on the road, he would see at least four fresh graves. But the lives were also lost to hunger, accidental shooting, exposure to elements, thirst, various accidents, and much else. The landscape was hostile as well. One stretch of the road was named Death Valley by the Argonauts. Previously, this place was known as Tomesha ("ground afire" in the languages of Both the Paiute and Panamint Shoshone Native American tribes). The name is appropriate, as it is one of the hottest places on Earth, comparable to the Sahara Desert. In summer, temperatures in Death Valley reach up to 134°F (56.7°C). To avoid heat strokes and dehydration, forty-niners had to climb the nearby mountains where the temperatures were cooler.

The Argonauts hoped that a better life awaited them in California. But the scene that greeted them was a gloomy one. The hills around the city were filled with tents, as the overcrowding pushed people out of San Francisco. Overcrowding also brought the cholera epidemic to the city, as well as pest infestation. Hunger was also ever-present, mainly due to inflated prices. Merchants profited the most from the Gold Rush. The demand for goods rose because so many people flocked to California, and merchants increased prices as a result. The inflation was so high that it became ridiculous. A shovel, the most wanted tool of the Gold Rush, reached the price of $36. That is approximately $1,000 today. The food prices were similar. A pound of cheese (0.45 kilograms) would sell for $26 ($700 today), and a bag of flour was $13 ($365 today). The inflated prices also affected hotels, where a room for a night would go for $250 a week. Many chose to rent only a sleeping space, without bedding and with many people lying next to you. The price of such a sleeping space was $8. Land prices also went up. A lot that was 150 feet wide (46 meters) sold for $8,000. Only one year earlier, this land would cost $20.

In 1850, San Francisco had five hundred rotting ships abandoned in its bay. The passengers, crew, and captains had run off to search for gold. The resourcefulness of the people prevailed, and some of the ships were pulled onshore to serve as housing, prisons, churches, and banks. San Francisco workers earned a dollar an hour. In the East, they would earn that much in a whole day. But many of them were paid in gold dust because there was not enough money circling. Merchants would also accept gold dust as payment if a customer had no money. Coins were so rare that their value increased, and the miners ended up paying a whole ounce of gold (31.1 grams) for one silver dollar. The real price of that much gold was sixteen dollars.

Mining camps sprouted all over the flows of the Sacramento, American, and Feather Rivers. The names of the camps were descriptive and sometimes funny, with examples such as Whiskey Bar, Skunk Gulch, and Dry Diggins. Miners who came with the dreams of getting rich often lost their gold on bets. Finding gold also wasn't as easy as the people were led to believe. It is estimated that only one in five forty-niners would be lucky enough to find some gold. The rest had to go back home empty-handed. But the opportunity was there; it just needed to be found. Among the first Argonauts were the five prospectors of the Yuba River. In just three months, they made over $75,000. At Sonora, a lump of gold weighing 28 pounds (12.7 kilograms) was found. In the same area, eight more nuggets weighing more than 20 pounds (9 kilograms) were found. And at the Coloma sawmill, the workers found gold each day, and its worth was anywhere between $20 and $30.

The first phase of the California Gold Rush was collecting the gold nuggets from the shallow waters of the rivers. The first prospectors used placer mining methods, which included techniques such as panning. They would shovel the dirt from the riverbed into a "washing pan," swirl it around to wash the pebbles and gravel, and pour the water off. Because gold is denser, it would remain at the bottom of the pan. During the California Gold Rush, many people used this technique as their only method of extracting gold from the river. But if they tried to discover gold in deeper streams, they would have to use more sophisticated equipment, such as a cradle or a rocker. These devices were 3 feet (0.9 meters) long, with riffles inside them. One miner would pour gravel in the cradle, while the other one would rock it to wash out debris. The gold was trapped against the riffles. There was a larger device called the "long tom," which was a kind of sluice box that was at least over 6 feet (1.8 meters) long. The river dirt was shoveled at one end of the device so the water would wash debris away, allowing the gold to remain trapped.

The gold panning technique is old; it dates from ancient Roman times. However, it is believed that it was introduced in California in 1848 by Isaac Humphrey, a miner from Georgia. The Mexicans developed their own panning technique with a flat dish called batea, and they might have actually brought the technique to California first. Nevertheless, panning was the most used method of gold mining during the California Gold Rush. It was a very slow method. A skillful miner would wash out fifty pans of river gravel during a twelve-hour workday. Even then, he would be lucky to obtain a few small nuggets of gold. Isaac Humphrey is also credited with the introduction of the cradle to California. Miners were capable of processing more river gravel with the cradle than with a pan. However, this device had its disadvantages, as it would fail to capture the smallest specks of gold in its riffles.

The easy pickings from the riverbeds ended in 1850. After that, there was simply no more gold to be found floating freely. What gold was left was locked in quartz deposits or were buried deep underground. When it came to the deposits, the miners resorted to building crushing mills. The quartz and rock had to be crumbled so that the gold could be extracted. But extraction wasn't simple. Mercury was used because it has the ability to trap gold. Then, the mercury would be melted and evaporated, leaving the gold free. These mercury vapors were poisonous, and gold extraction with this process was very dangerous.

Sometimes, the gold was simply too deep for common miners. They were unable to build or find the tools and equipment that could reach 50 feet (15.2 meters), as they were quite expensive. But if the gold vein was large, capitalists from the East would invest in the mines, and miners worked not for themselves but the investors. Soon, only big companies with expensive machines were left mining. They used huge dredges to sift through whole riverbeds, and they also used hydraulic mining techniques to force the water and gravel through narrow nozzles. Whole rivers, harbors, and farms were destroyed by this method of mining because large amounts of water, gravel, and dirt accumulated in the lowlands. Farmers were forced to move their cattle and fields or to fight the big corporations in courts so they could save their land.

The peak year of the California Gold Rush was 1852. In that year alone, companies excavated four million ounces (113,400 kilograms) of gold, which was worth eighty-one million dollars. The next year, they excavated seventy million dollars' worth of gold. But the amount of gold was declining, and between 1865 and 1885, they managed to earn between fifteen and twenty million dollars each year. The lowest amount was in 1900 when the mining companies earned only eleven million dollars. The largest amount of gold in California was found in the Sierra Nevada region, known as the Sierra Nevada goldfields. From the beginning of the Gold Rush up until the late 1890s, approximately 20 million ounces (620 tons) of gold were excavated here. In the north, the gold was found at the site of today's Yreka in 1851. The whole region became known as the Northern California goldfields. In 1848, near Nashville in El Dorado County, the term "Mother Lode" was used for the first time. It refers to the rich veins of gold that run through the limited territorial area.

Chapter 3 – The Labor Force

Gold Miners in California in 1850
https://en.wikipedia.org/wiki/California_Gold_Rush#/media/File:1850
_Woman_and_Men_in_California_Gold_Rush.jpg

Free miners remained in California until at least 1873, which is astonishing. Other mining states were completely capitalized by big corporations as soon as minerals and precious metals were discovered, but in California, a free miner, a common man, was the backbone of the whole system. The importance of the common man can also be seen in the abundance of evidence that comes directly from them. They left behind diaries, letters, and memoirs, which tell the everyday stories of the miners' lives. There are also ship records, newspaper articles, and reports from governmental agencies, which testify that ordinary people came to California in great numbers. But social and labor history is often disregarded as irrelevant when it comes to the Gold Rush, as this era was romanticized by historians and everyday people. The miners were represented not as a labor force but as adventurers seeking a better future. This is not completely untrue, but it is also not the only aspect of the laborer's endeavors. Because of this, it is important to get into the details and explain who the people were who joined the California Gold Rush. It is also important to find out how they lived and worked and how gold fever generated nationalism.

In just two years, from 1848 to 1850, California gained 300,000 people. They were all individual prospectors seeking the nuggets of gold in the California rivers or business owners moving to take advantage of this newly discovered market. In 1850, 75 percent of California's population were miners. But that number drastically fell ten years later, as the miners made up only 38 percent of California's workforce. It can be understood why the news of the discovery of gold would attract those who were already in the mining business, but it remains to be explained why so many people felt the urge to go and try a profession they had never practiced before. The first to arrive in California were miners from the British Isles, as well as experienced workers who came from the silver mines of Chile, Mexico, and Peru. But these new immigrants were only a fraction of the population that rushed to California. They were soon followed by Americans who had participated in earlier gold rushes in North Carolina and Georgia. Still, professional miners remained a minority.

Historians often blame newspapers for creating the gold fever. Journalists were more than eager to exaggerate the news of the discovery of gold in California, promising a quick fortune for everyone. At the time, agriculture in the northeastern US was in decline due to the rapid industrialization of the nation. Farms were no longer needed in such large numbers, as production had developed in big factories in the American cities. The people were destined to either struggle on failing farms or accept working in textile or shoe factories for a dollar a day. Promises of fortunes in the West were just too pleasing. At the time, egalitarian republicanism was on the rise, and the single-minded pursuit of wealth was encouraged by the political scene of the 19th-century United States. No wonder many were ready to take on the adventure and settle in the new western frontier. As we said earlier, the Gold Rush appealed to the poor, and they came in great numbers. However, they were never the poorest of the poor. They owned enough or had a family to borrow from so they could pay for the journey to California. The abject poor remained in the East, as they had no chances of gathering the $300 needed for the cheapest route to the West.

But not all who rushed to the West were motivated by the promise of gold. Faith, as well as the recently coined Manifest Destiny, drove a substantial amount of people to seek new horizons. The church needed to establish itself in the new frontier, a territory that had only recently been obtained from the Mexicans. And the ardent nationalists who firmly believed in the doctrine of Manifest Destiny, which stated that America was a God-given land, rushed to bring democracy and capitalism across the entire country. Unfortunately, with the ideology of Manifest Destiny came nationalism, and it was often used to justify harsh actions toward groups that were not European-American.

Although people seeking wealth were independent entrepreneurs, they were often forced to cooperate to build dams, dig tunnels, and reroute river flows. But even then, their cooperation was short, and partnerships were sparse. The labor practices in California during the Gold Rush era consisted of individual labor, North American slavery, Latin American peonage, and Chinese indentured labor. Blacks were a minority when it came to free private miners. They came as free men, often taking the abandoned ships that were supposed to sail to New England. However, a greater number of them came as employees or slaves of the wealthier white gold-seekers. There are no records that would confirm their numbers, but it is estimated by scholars that, by 1850, around two thousand miners were African American. At least 50 percent of them were slaves. It is a similar story with the Mexicans, but it is known they were much higher in number, probably around fifteen thousand. We will never know how many followed their patrons and were part of the unfree labor force. The Mexican patrons encouraged the movement of the peons, and they financed their transportation to California. The same patron system brought an unknown number of miners from other Latin American countries, such as Peru and Chile.

The Chinese were among the last to arrive. In 1850, the whole United States numbered about one thousand Chinese, and only five hundred of them were miners. But this changed in 1852 when, in just that year alone, twenty thousand Chinese entered California. However, the majority of the new Chinese immigrants were not miners but merchants. These merchants were often able to pay for their journey to North America. However, the miners coming from China were poor and couldn't afford the journey. Nevertheless, they accepted the credit system that was put in place by "middlemen." These prospectors would finance a miner's journey to North America, and the indebted miner would pay him back over time with the riches he gained there.

With so many nationalities flocking to California, nationalism and xenophobia were on the rise. The reasons were many. Americans preferred to have others working for them for free. If the minorities worked for foreign mining companies, they were seen as taking jobs away from those who lived in the nation, and they needed to be expelled or at least work for the American-born miners. Another reason was that the American miners were aware that the quantity of and access to gold. They observed the success of experienced miners from Latin America, and they resented them for it. To add fuel to the fire, the Mexican-American War ended in victory for the US, which helped reinvigorate Manifest Destiny ideology. Many Americans presumed that they had more rights to the gold in California than the defeated Mexicans. This also led to some violence against Europeans and Australians but not as much as against the colored people groups. Racism, which was prevalent even when the Mexicans oversaw the land, rose, especially when free miners turned to paid labor during the 1860s. It was known that the foreigners would work for less money, which led to their resentment by the white workers.

Foreign miners felt discrimination in legal terms too. In the 1850s, two new taxes for foreigners were implemented by the state legislature. The first tax targeted only Mexicans, and they had to pay $20 per month for a license to mine. The tax led to ten thousand Mexican miners abandoning their work and leaving California. The American merchants lost a significant number of their customers, and they rose in protest against this tax in 1851, which led to its repeal. By 1852, the influx of Chinese miners led to the implementation of another tax. This time, the amount was set to $3 per month. Later, it was raised to $4, an amount the Chinese were willing to pay. The Native Americans were not a target of these taxes, but they suffered the most violence of all the minority groups. At first, they were seen as a labor force to be used, and in 1848, they represented half of the miners in California. But the conditions of their lives and the fact that they were not paid for their work but instead given rations testifies that they were an unfree labor force.

Life in the Digging Sites

In the early years of the California Gold Rush, the equality people felt and promoted came from the idea that everyone had the same opportunity to find gold. All one needed was luck. And this was true for those early days, as the majority of miners were individual prospectors and worked with simple tools. They also felt some level of unity because working together allowed them to build bigger devices and wash out more river gravel and debris than if they panned alone. For the most part, they all dressed the same, in simple and dirty mining clothes, which erased the class differences between them. Their outfit also often consisted of heavy boots, a checked shirt, sturdy trousers, gloves, and a large belt that could hold tools. Thus, even clothing played a role in shaping the miners' identity. They were workers, proud to earn their fortunes by their sweat and blood. They often resented other occupational groups, such as doctors, lawyers, and merchants, even though they often depended on them. They regarded themselves as hardworking people, while the other professions were there to exploit their willingness to endure hardship.

The miners who came to California between 1848 and 1849 were either individuals or came with their families. By 1850, when there was no more gold to be easily picked with simple panning, the miners formed companies of four to eight people. Together, they would build cradles, dams, and sluices in order to be able to process more river gravel than before. The work was not only hard but also uncomfortable. Although the sun would burn the workers, they had to work in ice-cold waters that had accumulated from the melting snows of the mountain tops. The miners would take a break during the hottest hours of the day, but the work generally lasted from 6 a.m. until the sunlight was gone. The work was also seasonal, as there was no searching for gold during the winter when the rivers were frozen. That means the miners also felt a sense of urgency. They needed to find enough gold to sustain them through winter. They were able to wash 160 buckets of water every day to find one ounce of gold.

However, the miners had the option to go south for the winter, where the dry mines were. But even there, the period of effective work was very short, as the rains and bad weather would come in the springtime.

Digging sites were almost completely devoid of women. Men were forced to both work and care for food and other domestic necessities. They learned how to wash, sew, and cook. However, many people never acquired these skills and instead hired domestic-related services in the mining towns. Even in larger mining towns, such as Grass Valley and Nevada City, only one in every ten men were married during the 1860s. Among miners, the number of married men was even lower, with one per every twenty-five. Even though the number of women in California was small, they had their own role to play during the Gold Rush era, which you can read about more in the next chapter.

A miner's diet often consisted of bread, meat, biscuits, and coffee. Fresh fruit and vegetables were rare. Although transport lines developed over time, domestic vegetables and fruits were the only ones the miners ate, and they were consumed for a very short seasonal period. Miners didn't lack food, but many of them still starved. This was due to price inflation. Also, with the dietary deficiencies and the lack of minerals and nutrients acquired from fresh food, people suffered diarrhea, scurvy, and dysentery. After 1850, the situation improved somewhat, as the development of large mining companies invested in better food transportation.

Other diseases quickly spread through the mining towns due to the hastily erected primitive houses, which were unclean and offered little protection from the elements. Most miners lived in canvas tents, but some built log cabins. After 1850, the mining towns began to be established, and the situation improved. But even then, these early towns were mostly made of rudimentary cabins. It was only after the 1870s that they started building proper brick houses.

But none of this stopped the movement of the miners. They worked for five months and then would retreat to cities such as Sacramento, San Francisco, or Stockton for the winter. The miners often needed to find jobs during the winter months because many of them had no luck in finding any gold. Even during the mining season, they would constantly move, trying to find spots rich with gold.

From Adventurers to Wage Laborers

The glory days of the forty-niners, Argonauts, and adventurers were short-lived. Those who caught the gold fever early, in 1849, were still able to make a fortune by collecting gold from the rivers of California. By 1850, their luck started to turn, and they had to lose their independence to survive. During the 1850s, the Argonauts worked as wage laborers for corporations that employed hundreds of people. At first, the corporations sought to attract experienced miners, and they targeted those who came from abroad, especially the British Isles. But very soon, in just a few years, they started employing anyone interested in trying their luck in finding gold. Of course, some of the first Argonauts were lucky and managed to get rich practically overnight. But most of them had no such luck, and they had to accept reality. To survive, they had to accept regular wages. Soon, they were working for similar prices and under similar conditions like factory workers in the East.

Because the companies sought to employ more and more miners, the wages dropped by half in just one year. The foreign experts were being paid $20 a day back in 1848 and 1849. But when the companies started employing just any forty-niner, the wages dropped to $10 a day. Three years later, the wage was $5, and in the late 1850s, it was only $3. The decline in wages mainly occurred because the cost of living started declining too. In the early 1860s, only one in ten miners owned some property. Merchants and businessmen, on the other hand, lived much better lives. For the most part, they owned their own properties and were family-oriented men.

Chapter 4 – Women in the California Gold Rush

Women in a brothel in San Francisco during the Gold Rush era
https://en.wikipedia.org/wiki/Women_in_the_California_Gold_Rush
#/media/File:Early_San_Francisco_prostitutes.jpg

Of all the immigrants who rushed from the East Coast to California during the early days of the Gold Rush, only 3 percent were women. The whole mythic and historical narrative of the California Gold Rush is oriented on men, their endeavors, adventures, and hardship. But women were, although in much smaller numbers, a contributing factor to the mining communities. They worked the goldfields alongside men, cared for children or the sick, maintained boarding houses, and entertained. Sometimes, they even earned more than their husbands. Women saw prospects in California and were attracted to a freedom that was impossible back in the East. Some were brave and adventurous, while others were gentle and caring. Women of all professions and races made up the diverse mining communities. They were pioneers, settlers, and pillars of family and society.

Women emigrants often wrote diaries and letters back home, and these are some of the best sources that historians have at their disposal in understanding the hardships people went through to reach the new frontier. From these writings, we can often learn how the mining communities lived and developed over time. Some of these women were even journalists, working for the newspapers back in the East. Their task was to follow men and report on life in California. But whether they were housewives, entertainers, or journalists, these women wrote eloquently, their writing sometimes filled with humor.

The first women to collect gold in California were Mexican and Native American women, as they were already there when the gold was first found. Many labored as slaves, although sometimes they were free women panning for gold alongside their families. Even children were involved in the search for gold, both boys and girls. These families were established in California long before it became a part of the US. Californian Mexicans were called Californios, and women played a very important social role in their communities. Once the Anglo-Americans and Europeans started arriving in California, they sought to marry Californio women, as they realized they would open the door to the already established high society of California.

Californio women didn't work the goldfields, but they were an integral part of the miners' lives. They were the mistresses of the estates, and they were respected and often romanticized.

The first wave of miners also brought the first major wave of Anglo-American women to California as early as 1849. Some of them simply couldn't let go of their husbands, and they decided to come along. Other women were struck by gold fever and wanted to take their own chances at creating their fortunes. Among the earliest women to arrive in California were the entertainers. They were dancers, singers, actresses, and prostitutes. They were well aware of the scarcity of women in California, and they wanted to capitalize on it. Most of them were already experienced in these lines of work, as they had worked in theaters, saloons, dance halls, or brothels in other cities and even other countries.

For instance, when the California gold fever hit France, many French miners came, but so did women, who were quickly employed in saloons to serve drinks or in gambling houses to rake the winnings. They were paid well, up to $250 a week. However, these women would quickly marry merchants or businessmen who brought their companies to California. The first French women were considered to be of "good character," as they rarely indulged in prostitution. But they were followed by a bigger company of ladies from France, which consisted of various characters. In 1850, the *Pacific News*, a newspaper from San Francisco, wrote that nine hundred French women were expected to arrive.

But French women were not the only ones to come. They may have been pioneers, but soon, ladies from all over the world started arriving. Most were Chilean, Peruvian, and Australian women who followed their husbands or came to work as prostitutes. They were the first to settle the mining towns near gold-bearing rivers, and they quickly prospered. One Anglo-American prostitute claimed she managed to earn $50,000 in just two months. But while these free women, for the most part, earned money by their own free will and choice, Native American women were seen as lower creatures, and they were often raped and passed around for free. Many of the other women didn't sympathize with the Native Americans. They mocked them and refused to help or treat them when they were injured or sick.

Enos Christman, a journalist and publisher from Pennsylvania who came to the goldfields in 1849, wrote how all the women he met had low morals, were constantly drunk, and served men's pleasure. He also wrote that meeting a good woman who was capable of reading and writing was almost impossible. He only personally met several ladies in California who were "good" and had families. He also claimed that all the foreign women who came to California were prostitutes. But Christman's words were not how other men felt about these first women. Miners actively sought the company of women, and they didn't consider them immoral.

During the early part of the Gold Rush era, there were no laws that regulated sex workers, and many madams were able to earn a fortune by opening and maintaining brothels. Most women who came to California during those early days had no money for the journey. Nevertheless, ships accepted them and expected them to pay for their trip upon arrival. This was no problem at all, as the saloons, brothels, and gambling halls gladly employed them and even paid their debt for the ship ticket. The girls would work off the price in three to six months. But ships also accepted women without money because they could advertise themselves as "having girls onboard" in order to attract male Argonauts to come and sail with them. Women were so valuable and scarce that men were willing to pay $20 just for the privilege to sit at the same table as the lady.

When it comes to the prostitutes in California, there was a hierarchy in terms of value. The fairer the skin they had, the more worthy they were deemed. Anglo-American, French, and other European girls were highly sought, and they were the most expensive prostitutes, often reserved for wealthy businessmen. In popularity,

Latino women came next, followed by the Chinese. Chinese women were at the bottom, but only because the Native American women weren't worth any money at all. Chinese women were also very rare, especially at the beginning of the Gold Rush era. By 1850, there were only seven of them in the whole San Francisco area. The first Chinese prostitute to arrive is believed to be the famous Ah Toy, who arrived in 1849. She initially sailed with her husband, but he died during the voyage, so she found herself completely alone in the new land. Luckily, she had some money saved, and she started her own brothel, importing girls from China, often as young as eleven. Ah Toy became famous not only for being the first Asian prostitute in California but also because she was brave and able to defend herself and her business from Anglo-American and Chinese men who sought to control her.

Women of good reputation came right after the "entertainers." Most of the women would take the Isthmus of Panama route, as it was the fastest and least dangerous. They traveled either with their husbands or in groups of other women who were also on their way to meet their husbands, who had settled in California at an earlier date. Some of them complained of the conditions of the journey, but they all displayed an iron will and a determination to finish their route. Some of them were fully independent and alone, struck by the gold fever themselves, hoping they could become miners and find their fortunes. Some women sailed around Cape Horn, but they were in the minority. Yet, we know about them, for we can see their names in the ship logs. The poorest, but also perhaps the bravest women, were those who crossed the land route to California. They were seldom alone, always accompanied by their husbands and children. Sometimes, though, their husbands were waiting for them in California, in which case it would just be the women and children. Some of them even dared to start a journey with babies. The stories from their diaries are sometimes hard to read, as they described the hardships of crossing Death Valley.

These women who crossed the plains in covered wagons had a lot to tell. Some of them were even celebrated as heroes because they were brave enough to stand by their men when their caravans were attacked by Native American tribes. They cared for the sick, buried the dead, and counted graves. Their diaries often describe how they had to leave oxen, horses, dogs, and sometimes even men behind in order to increase their chances of survival. Catherine Haun wrote of how her family had to abandon their dog, who was so exhausted from heat and thirst that he couldn't take another step. She later found out that the family who was traveling in a wagon behind them took the dog and ate it. Food was sparse, but water even more so.

Juliet Brier was one of the first women to cross Death Valley in 1849. She traveled with her husband, a reverend of the Methodist church who embarked on the journey to spread the faith to the West. The Brier family arrived in Salt Lake City too late in the season and couldn't cross the Sierra Nevada mountain range. They decided not to hesitate in Salt Lake City and instead continued west, taking an alternative road known as the Old Spanish Trail. But once they came to present-day Enterprise in Utah, they decided to split off from the main caravan and join a different group of one hundred wagons that were willing to try a route they had learned about from a passer-by. Allegedly, this was a shortcut and should have brought them to California much sooner. They followed a makeshift map that showed Walker Pass, but the map itself wasn't reliable. The Brier family and their party missed the mountain pass and continued walking west in what was to become the most horrible part of their journey, a desert with hardly any water sources and without a path for their wagons. They were forced to continue on foot, with some animals but no wagons. Most of the animals they had to kill and turn into jerky so they had enough food for the road ahead. Juliet was said to have done most of the work. She walked and carried her three children (all under eight years old) so they wouldn't slow down the party. She labored and cared for her family, and she was the only reason they all survived the horrors of Death Valley and made it to California. She nursed the sick, took care of the animals, and cooked. Other travelers remembered her as the "best man of their party."

Chapter 5 – The Golden State

San Francisco 1850/1851
https://en.wikipedia.org/wiki/California_Gold_Rush#/media/File:SanFranciscoharbor1851c_sharp.jpg

When the United States acquired California from Mexico, it did not immediately become a state. But once gold was discovered, people began to flock in droves, and the citizens of California wanted to control their future. In these early days, California was administered by Congress, but it was unable to control the people, so a local government was needed to implement a system of law and order. Even US President Zachary Taylor (served 1849–1850) urged the people to apply for statehood. By late 1849, the residents of California voted to become a state. But a major main question remained: What kind of a state would it be? A free state or a slave state? After all, over two thousand African Americans came to settle in California, and up until that point, they were considered to be free. Although racism was strong in the mining camps, some of them chose to stay. The majority settled in larger cities, where prejudice against them wasn't so obvious.

The Congress passionately debated about California's status, and in 1850, they came up with the Compromise of 1850. Finally, California could enter the Union as a free state. On September 9th, 1850, California officially became the thirty-first state of the United States of America. However, racism persisted even though California became one of the most progressive states in the US. For instance, Californios had been respected by the European-Americans when the territory belonged to Mexico. But now that it was a US territory, the Spanish-speaking people suffered heavy discrimination. Anyone with a darker shade of skin was perceived as unwanted. Besides having to pay foreign mining taxes, the Californios lost their ranches, as the European-Americans took them over and divided them into smaller farms. Mexicans were considered naturalized citizens, but that didn't matter; they were still forced to pay the foreign mining tax, just as anyone else coming to search for gold in the US. They also had to endure lynchings, beatings, and robberies. This all led to many Californios leaving the goldfields by the end of 1850 and going south to Mexico.

The Chinese were also discriminated against heavily. There weren't many of them during the initial years of the Gold Rush, but by the late 1850s, they numbered around twenty-five thousand. They spoke little English and were not Christians. This was enough for the European-Americans to think of them as suspicious and not trustworthy. The Chinese were often accused of stealing and of intentionally destroying campsites. In 1854, a proposal to keep the Chinese from arriving in the US was put forward, but it didn't pass. However, around twenty years later, Congress finally passed the law through which the immigration of some Chinese people was stopped. With the Page Act of 1875, Chinese women were banned from migrating to the US. This was the first-ever federal immigration law implemented in the United States. The intention was to stop the influx of cheap labor, but it targeted only women because they were thought to have loose morals. In 1882, a new law was implemented, the Chinese Exclusion Act, by which both men and women of China were banned from immigrating to the US.

But the Native Americans in California perhaps had the saddest fate. They numbered around 300,000 before the arrival of the European-Americans. The Chumash were the largest group, with over ten thousand members. Although the Native Americans who occupied California belonged to different tribes and were culturally and linguistically distinct from each other, they rarely engaged in tribal wars. Instead, they lived in peace, at least for the most part, and shared the land, with the different tribes adapting to living in different regions. When the first Spanish and Mexican missions came to California in 1769, they had but one goal: to introduce Christianity to the indigenous peoples. However, the Spanish rule was devastating for the Native Americans. During the Mexican regime, most tribes died out due to various diseases that had been imported from Europe. Violence was also not uncommon, and modern historians believe that these Christian missionaries treated natives as little more than slaves.

Once California became a state, the federal authorities essentially made the extermination of Native Americans legal. They even financed it, and many settlers, miners, and farmers joined in. When the news of the extermination of Native Americans reached other parts of the world, there was no reaction. In fact, in 1850, the California authorities came up with the Act for the Government and Protection of Indians by which the white settlers could legally take Native American children from their parents. The intention was to apprentice these children and integrate them into American society. In reality, they were used as free labor. Children were not the only ones who were forced to work for free either. Around twenty-seven thousand adult natives labored for free, as they had no money to pay the alleged bonds or bails for crimes that they often didn't commit. Even though California was a free state on paper, what they did to the Native Americans is considered a form of legalized slavery.

Most of the Native American deaths were recorded between 1846 and 1873. More than 370 massacres took place during this period. Men, women, and children were killed by death squads that were formed from local militias and financed by the state. But the first two years of the California Gold Rush were the hardest. More than 100,000 Native Americans were killed or chased away from their land. Some of them tried emigrating to the north, but there are no records of what happened to them. The US government approved and financed more than 1,500 raids on Native Americans. To avoid mass killings, some tribes agreed to relocate to reservations. This was the fate of the Yokut tribe that inhabited the area around the Fresno River. But many tribes refused to be taken away from their land. The Yosemite tribe persisted the longest, as they inhabited the territory of what is today known as Yosemite National Park for centuries. But when the government captured the Yosemite chieftain in 1851 and killed his son, he finally agreed to sign a treaty and bring his people out of the mountains to the reservation dedicated to them.

The first apology for these crimes against humanity that had been committed in California during the 19th century came from California Governor Gavin Newsom. In 2019, he proclaimed that the massacres that took place were indeed genocide and that they should be described as such in history books.

However, the Native Americans were not only legally persecuted and killed; they also suffered the loss of their land. The ecological impact of mining is not to be underestimated. The Native Americans mainly thrived as hunters and gatherers. They lived in nature, and the environment was incredibly important for their survival. Due to the excessive mining, the landscape of the Sierra Nevada changed. Toxic waste was released into the rivers, killing fish. The animals that Native Americans depended on, such as buffalos, deer, and rabbits, disappeared from the region, which led to starvation.

Chapter 6 – The Significance of the California Gold Rush on the Global Economy

The timing of the discovery of gold in California is probably what propelled the United States to become one of the driving economic forces in the world. For most people, the mention of January 24th, 1848, means nothing; the date itself is not even commemorated in the state. However, that is when it is thought James Marshall found his first gold nugget in California, setting the stage for great events to happen. At the same time, the American nation was about to feel the impact of growing industrialization. The Industrial Revolution was already happening in Europe, and it moved its way toward the fairly new country, transforming it from an agrarian society into an industrial giant.

Looking at the larger picture, one can see the California Gold Rush was crucial for triggering economic changes in the country. Because of the large influx of gold, the US economy significantly accelerated. The result was the creation of new businesses and banks, as well as new governmental financial institutions. Agricultural expansion was stimulated too, and the volume of trade and commerce grew. New forms of transportation were also needed, which only served to further boost industries.

The Gold Rush moved many people across the US, but not all of them were miners or adventurers who sought to turn their luck by finding gold. Many of them rushed to California to start new business ventures or open new service industries and manufacturing. Food, clothing, mining, hardware, and all kinds of luxuries were needed in California. When mining methods changed from panning to excavation, heavy machinery was needed. In under one decade, the Northern Californians started their own iron industry. They manufactured steam engines, hydraulic pumps, and stamp mills. By 1861, more than one thousand people worked in the production of mining equipment in San Francisco alone. Powder works were opened in California as early as 1855, completely replacing the imported explosives the people had relied upon.

Gold mining demanded other industries as well. Lumber was needed, not only for house building but also for the support beams of mines. Just one decade after the beginning of the California Gold Rush, Humboldt and Mendocino Counties were producing over thirty-five million board feet per year. As for food, California was quick to establish flour mills. It had none when the Gold Rush began back in 1848, but by the 1860s, two hundred mills were in operation. California produced enough flour to feed its people and export it to Japan, China, and parts of Europe. Due to the rapid increase of people, the clothing industry bloomed. Most notable are the Mission Woolen Mills, which became the largest producers of cloth in the West, and Levi Strauss, who, together with Jacob Davis, invented the fashionable blue jeans. At first, these riveted pants were made for miners since they were sturdy enough to endure the hard working conditions. Over the centuries, they became a fashion staple across the world. Farming was another industry that bloomed. Many miners who weren't successful in finding gold turned to growing fruit and vegetables or running dairy farms. They produced enough food to cover the whole Pacific Coast region.

But the Gold Rush wasn't only a local economic event. The products made in California were exported around the world. During the California Gold Rush, in 1853, Commodore Matthew Perry opened the Japanese ports to trade with the United States. California, being in the West, benefited greatly from the newly established contacts. In general, California's farm products were highly valued in Asia, and San Francisco merchants enjoyed great success in trade with China and Japan.

The influence of the California Gold Rush on Europe was less significant, but it could still be felt. Norway, whose economy completely depended on transportation, trade, and commerce, was probably influenced the most by the economic growth of California and the US. It recognized the possibilities in the newly emerging economy of the Pacific Coast and stressed the importance of building a canal across the Isthmus of Panama. The iron manufacturers of Norway also saw the potential new market in California for railways and railroad equipment. France was also influenced by the Gold Rush on a deeper level. Thousands of people saw the opportunity to settle and start their own businesses in California. Many young people gave up on the revolution that raged in France in 1848 and went to search for new job opportunities in the US. But once Napoleon III established political stability in France in 1852, the immigration to America ebbed. One million Germans emigrated to the US during the Gold Rush, and 300,000 of them settled in California. Many Germans established themselves as farmers and/or started grocery businesses. And when it came to Great Britain, around fifty thousand skilled miners came to California during the 1850s. More than 500,000 British immigrants followed. During the early years of the Gold Rush, British stock companies invested over ten million dollars in California's mining companies. They didn't earn much, but they established their presence in California, which allowed them to expand their interests. Soon, the stock companies of Great Britain started investing in California's developing industries, and they helped propel the local iron and food production.

The influx of California's gold into the world markets created price spikes in Europe. The costs of goods increased all over the world, but it was most significantly felt in California itself, as well as in Great Britain. However, the influx of people in California demanded increased imports, and Great Britain was ready to fulfill those demands. Between 1850 and 1855, British exports to California numbered around $2 million per year. These booming exports brought new prosperity to the British Isles, and the economic stability brought increased demands for workers and the rise of wages. So, even though the prices were rising, most people had no trouble earning the necessary money to survive.

In the Pacific Rim countries, the California Gold Rush caused a shortage of workers. Many Hawaiian sugar plantation workers left for California, hoping to find employment in the goldfields. A similar thing happened in China, where people decided to leave for either California or Hawaii (where they sought to fill the empty sugar plantations). However, it should be noted that the Gold Rush coincided with the Taiping Rebellion, a civil war that caused famine and the loss of properties in China. Thus, it is no wonder so many people had to leave their home country and seek fortune elsewhere.

Due to the hype of the California Gold Rush, people tried to find precious metals in South Africa and Australia, and they were successful, further adding to the influx of gold to the world's economy.

Conclusion

January 24th, 1848, is the approximate date given to the discovery of gold in California. James Wilson Marshall, the man who first found gold near Sutter's Mill, was never certain what date he found that first nugget. Later in life, he said he thought it was January 19th, but several other accounts contradict Marshall's claim. Some historians even believe it wasn't Marshall who found the gold in the first place but an unknown Native American mill worker. This Native American is remembered as "Indian Jim," and according to the story, he gave the gold nugget, which was the size of a brass button, to a white mill worker who later showed it to Marshall. The problem here is not that we don't know how it exactly happened but the lack of evidence itself. There were only a few witnesses to the discovery of gold and even fewer records about it. Everyone who was involved in finding that first gold nugget was a commoner, an uneducated person with little to no incentive to describe the events in the written word.

Even though the California Gold Rush is not an event that is commemorated in the US, it is certainly an event that shaped the country. The massive influx of immigrants into the US, as well as the influx of California's gold into the economy, defined the world's history of the period. Previously sparsely populated regions now had to organize a state and become part of the US. To keep in touch with the families these immigrants had left behind, the United States had to invest in the development of communication, infrastructure, and transportation. The distance between California and the rest of the US had to be bridged. But it was the people who came to California that started the state's production industry, agriculture, and the many small and large businesses.

The importance of the discovery of gold on the development of California is still seen in its modern symbols. The state's motto is "Eureka," an ancient Greek word that means "I have found it." The state is still nicknamed the Golden State, but it no longer symbolizes only the Gold Rush. Instead, this nickname today means that California is a place of prosperity, new beginnings, and hope. Route 49, which runs through the Sierra Nevada foothills, is aptly named after the forty-niners, a brave generation that pioneered the Gold Rush. Also, the sign of Route 49 is shaped like a miner's spade to commemorate all those people who ventured to California in search of gold.

Here's another book by Captivating History that you might like

Free Bonus from Captivating History (Available for a Limited time)

Hi History Lovers!

Now you have a chance to join our exclusive history list so you can get your first history ebook for free as well as discounts and a potential to get more history books for free! Simply visit the link below to join.

Captivatinghistory.com/ebook

Also, make sure to follow us on Facebook, Twitter and Youtube by searching for Captivating History.

References

Altman, Linda Jacobs. *The California Gold Rush in American History*. Enslow Publishers, 1997.

Caughey, John Walton and W. R. Cameron. *The California Gold Rush*. University of California Press, 1975.

"Graphs Showing Miners' Wages and Value of Gold Production, 1848-1860 · SHEC: Resources for Teachers." *Social History for Every Classroom*, shec.ashp.cuny.edu/items/show/1738.

Marks, Paula Mitchell. *Precious Dust: The American Gold Rush Era, 1848-1900*. W. Morrow, 1994.

Morison, Samuel Eliot. *The Oxford History of the American People*. Oxford University Press, 1965.

Sonneborn, Liz. *The California Gold Rush: Transforming the American West*. Chelsea House Publishers, 2009.

Stanley, Jerry. *Digger: The Tragic Fate of the California Indians from the Missions to the Gold Rush*. Crown Publishers, Inc., 1997.

White, Stewart Edward. *The Forty-Niners: A Chronicle of the California Trail and El Dorado*. Yale Univ. Press, 1921.

www.ingramcontent.com/pod-product-compliance
Lightning Source LLC
LaVergne TN
LVHW042003060526
838200LV00041B/1855